Annalee, Briana, and Caiden..... Go to Paris France!

ABC Explorers

by Lauren Rosa

AuthorHouse™
1663 Liberty Drive
Bloomington, IN 47403
www.authorhouse.com
Phone: 1 (800) 839-8640

Published by AuthorHouse 10/06/2016

ISBN: 978-1-5246-3953-2 (sc)
ISBN: 978-1-5246-3954-9 (hc)
ISBN: 978-1-5246-3952-5 (e)

Library of Congress Control Number: 2016915192

Printed in the USA

authorHOUSE®

Annalee, Briana, and Caiden
Wanted to be just like their Mom and Dad.
Their parents have traveled the world
From Tokyo to Bagdad.
With their parents usually away
Their imaginations ran wild.
Caiden would always invent things
He was no ordinary child.

As the girls sat in front of the window
Looking out at the rainy day
Briana thought to herself
"I wonder if it's raining far away."
Just then, she had a great idea
That would change their life indeed.
She got a pen and paper
And wrote down what they would need.

"Caiden! Anna! I have such a great idea
Please let me know what your thoughts are.
It's a combination of a rocket, boat, and car
We can call it the "Rocabar!"
They all wanted to explore the world
Just as their parents have done.
And the Rocabar was the first of its' kind.
It'd be the only one.

"I think it's a great idea!
We will get started right away.
We would need to hurry up though
It's almost the end of May."
Together they gathered everything
They needed for this masterpiece.
Caiden said "We can't build this indoors."
Anna replied "Well, the rain has stopped at least."

They worked around the clock
And didn't stop till it was done.
They barely had time to sleep
Because they were having so much fun!
After all the excitement
Of finalizing their creation
They needed all the sleep they could get
Before traveling around the nation.

Early the next morning
Briana rolled off Caiden's back.
"Hey guys! Wake up! It's morning now!
Let's go inside and pack!"
Annalee wakes up stretching
And glad it's morning too.
She asks as she grew more curious
"So now where are we off too?"

Just then the room darkens
As the clouds start rolling in.
Now here comes the rain
Followed by the thunder and lightning.
Bri states "This is one of the things
I will not miss while we're away.
I know its really beneficial
But it seems to rain everyday."

Annalee, Briana, and Caiden are packed
And ready to head to France
In their newly invented Rocabar
Now they had their chance
To become explorers like their Mom and Dad
Who have traveled near and far
Now it's their turn to do the same
They feel like they can reach the stars.

As they turn the key and start it up
They can hear the engine roar
It's like music to their ears
As the skies they are ready to soar.
Up, up, and away, they begin to incline
"There's no turning back now."
Briana says with a smile on her face
"I just advise you not to look down."

They begin to fly over the Atlantic Ocean
Headed straight for Paris, France.
As they arrive, people are flooding the streets
And they think "Wow! What is the chance?!"
They saw aircraft galore and soldiers on horses
The tanks were not far behind.
They were celebrating Bastille Day
And the parade was one of a kind!

"We have to land this thing and join in on the fun!"
"But the only question now is where?"
They looked all around for an empty spot.
Then Bri yells "Look over there!"
She found a perfect spot
They parked underneath a tree.
And just their luck
They were in front of the Palace de L'Elysee!

This is where the President of France
Throws a garden party each year.
Everywhere they look, there's people dancing
And smiles from ear to ear.
They began dancing in the streets
And mingling with the crowd.
That's when this nice couple
Offered to show them around.

"We are traveling the world
And this is actually our first stop.
Whatever information you can share about France
We would appreciate a lot!"
"Of course, we would love to help
And for now, right here we should stay.
We wouldn't want you to miss
The beautiful fireworks display!"

"There's the famous Eiffel Tower.
The most visited monument to this day.
Did you know that with a strong gust of wind
Up to 15 centimeters it can sway?
Gustave Eiffel built it using iron,
So no one's ever gotten a splinter.
And I'm sure you didn't know
It shrinks six inches in the winter!"

"How do the French greet each other?
We hug or we shake hands."
"Well we kiss from cheek to cheek
To our family and friends.
If you guys want to stop and eat
A tasty French tradition,
You should definitely try a crepe."
"Oh that's just what I've been wishing!"

The crepes smelled so good
So they all sat down to eat.
"Do you know the French started the tradition
Of decorating the Christmas tree?
They originally used flowers and apples,
Until the apple harvest died.
Then a glass blower made some bulbs
And the tradition spread worldwide!"

"France has so many types of cheese
It could puzzle Mickey Mouse!
Over 400 kinds and counting
Sometimes I lose count.
We use milk from three different animals.
The cow, the goat, or the sheep.
All of this talk is making my mouth water
Let's go get some cheese!"

"The French really love their cheese
And it goes just great with wine."
Bri asks "What exactly is this wine
That goes with cheese just fine?"
"It's a drink that's made with grapes
And we have over 300 different kinds.
And we have just as many vineyards
Where the grapes all grow on vines."

"Wow, so food is really important to you
As you have just explained.
And the food is so delicious
There's no need to complain."
"I'm glad you have enjoyed it
And just one more thing before you go,
It's about something in the United States
That not too many people know."

"In the late 1800's
A very long time ago,
France gave the U.S. the Statue of Liberty
As a sign of friendship they wanted to show.
Gustave Eiffel built this statue as well
With brown copper that is now unseen.
Because when the copper mixes with salt water
It turned the statue green!"

"Wow. We cannot thank you enough
For what you've taught us so far."
They all thanked the very nice couple.
"But now we have to head back to the Rocabar.
We must continue our journey
And around the world we will go.
Who knows, maybe our next stop
Could even be Tokyo!"